RECYCLABLES

Gareth Stevens Publishing

A WORLD ALMANAC EDUCATION GROUP COMPANY

Please visit our web site at: www.garethstevens.com
For a free color catalog describing Gareth Stevens Publishing's
list of high-quality books and multimedia programs,
call 1-800-542-2595 (USA) or 1-800-387-3178 (Canada).
Gareth Stevens Publishing's fax: (414) 332-3567.

Library of Congress Cataloging-in-Publication Data

Recyclables.
        p. cm. — (Let's create!)
    Includes bibliographical references.
    Summary: Provides step-by-step instructions for turning egg cartons,
cardboard tubes, frozen food containers, and other disposable materials
into craft projects, including easy variations.
    ISBN 0-8368-4018-6 (lib. bdg.)
    1. Handicraft—Juvenile literature.   2. Recycling (Waste, etc.)—Juvenile
literature. [1. Handicraft. 2. Recycling—Waste.] I. Title. II. Series.
TT160.M3813   2004
745.5—dc22   2003057358

This North American edition first published in 2004 by
Gareth Stevens Publishing
A World Almanac Education Group Company
330 West Olive Street, Suite 100
Milwaukee, WI 53212 USA

First published as *¡Vamos a crear! Materiales de reciclaje* with an original copyright
© 2001 by Parramón Ediciones, S.A., – World Rights, text and illustrations by Parramón's
Editorial Team. This U.S. edition copyright © 2004 by Gareth Stevens, Inc. Additional
end matter copyright © 2004 by Gareth Stevens, Inc.

English Translation: Colleen Coffey
Gareth Stevens Series Editor: Dorothy L. Gibbs
Gareth Stevens Designer: Katherine A. Goedheer

Printed in Spain

1 2 3 4 5 6 7 8 9 08 07 06 05 04

Table of Contents

Introduction

Cardboard egg cartons and paper towel tubes; plastic cups, bottles, and frozen food containers; milk and juice cartons and cans; cork bottle stoppers; and Styrofoam trays are part of an almost endless list of objects that people throw away every day. We dispose of these objects because the function for which they were made has been completed. We have already used them to store food, to wrap presents, to protect fragile objects, and so on. Most of these throwaway materials, however, can be reused in other ways. The process of reusing disposable materials is called recycling. Materials that can be recycled are called recyclables.

Many recyclables can be used to make fun crafts. How many times have you had to go out and buy cartons, boxes, wrapping paper, or other materials for your craft projects? Taking advantage of used supplies is a great way to develop your imagination as you give new shapes to objects that seemed to be useless. When you use recyclables, however, always take into consideration the condition and cleanliness of the recycled material after its first use.

This book will give you ideas for making original crafts. You can use a juice or milk carton to make a cow container for storing small objects, or you can turn an egg carton into a palm tree or a plastic pudding cup into the nose of a baby bear. Each of this book's twelve fun-to-make projects will help you recognize the many possible uses for recyclables. You can complete these crafts following the easy, illustrated, step-by-step instructions. Better yet, after looking at the projects and the materials they use, you can invent your own craft projects!

To make almost any creation with recyclables, you will need some basic art and craft supplies, in addition to the recycled objects. Your basic supplies will include scissors, tape, glue, string, colored pencils, paints, markers, and more.

Watch for special instructions at the end of each project to try other great ideas. Sometimes, making just one small change creates a very different result.

**Don't wait! Start today.
Make clever crafts
from throwaways.**

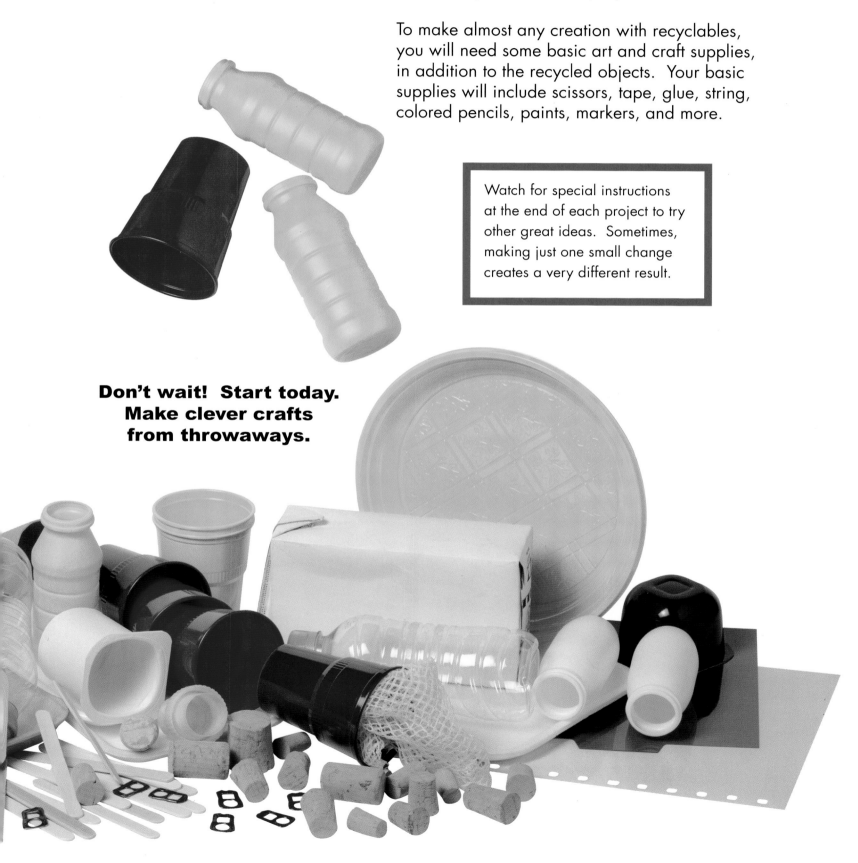

Deep Blue Sea Scene

You don't need an aquarium, or even a fishbowl, to surround yourself with sea life. This colorful fish scene is almost as good as the real thing. Of course, Styrofoam fish can't swim, but watch how cleverly they move!

1 Tear light and dark blue tissue paper into small pieces. Dilute white glue with water. Brush the diluted glue onto the pieces of tissue paper and press them onto a Styrofoam tray.

2 On another Styrofoam tray, draw three different types of fish with a black marker. Trace over the outlines of the fish with a clay pick, then cut them out.

You will need:
- light blue and dark blue tissue paper
- white glue
- paintbrushes
- 2 Styrofoam trays
- black marker
- clay pick
- scissors
- different colors of paint
- round toothpicks

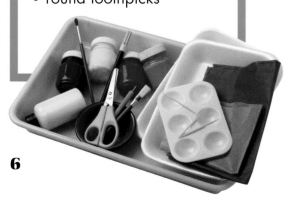

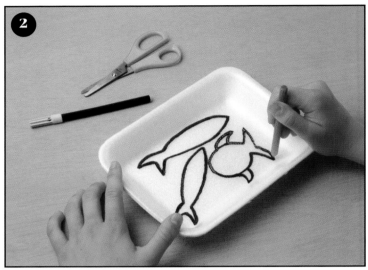

3 Paint each of the three fish a different color and decorate each fish in a different style, such as stripes, spots, or swirls.

4 Stick a toothpick into the center of each fish, on the back side.

5 Stick the fish onto the paper-covered tray, anywhere you want them to be.

Move the fish around whenever you like — or make more fish so you can change your sea scene!

Another Great Idea!
Make just one large figure, such as an octopus, and stick it into the center of the paper-covered tray.

Cow Container

When the milk is gone, turn the carton into this cute cow. It makes a dandy candy container.

You will need:
- scissors
- milk carton
- white poster board
- black marker
- colored pencils
- glue stick
- clay pick
- twine

1 Use a pair of scissors to cut off the top of a clean, dry milk carton.

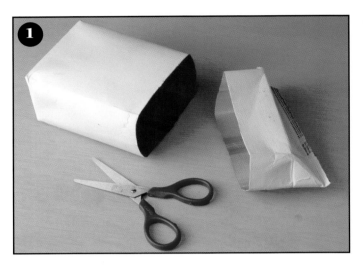

2 Cut a piece of white poster board in half, across the width. On one half, draw black spots with a black marker and make green grass across the bottom with a colored pencil.

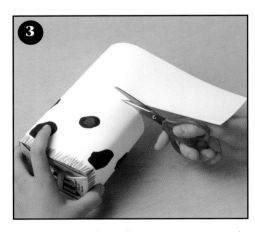

3 Wrap the drawing around the bottom of the carton and glue it on with glue stick. Cut off any extra poster board.

4 On the other half of the white poster board, draw the front and back of a cow and cut out the shapes.

5 Color both parts of the cow with black marker and colored pencils.

6 Glue the front and back parts of the cow onto opposite sides of the covered carton.

How now? A cow! And you have reused a milk carton. Now, put something special inside of it.

7 Poke a hole into the back of the cow with a clay pick. Thread a piece of twine through the hole to make the cow's tail.

Another Great Idea!
Draw a lion or an elephant or any other animal you like.

Painted Palm

Cut apart an egg carton and use the pieces to make a palm tree. Painting the palm makes it look almost lifelike.

You will need:

- scissors
- cardboard egg carton (for 6 eggs) with a flat top
- clay pick
- orange and green paints
- paintbrush
- thin, flexible wire

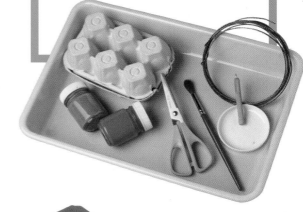

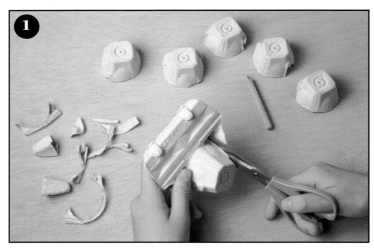

1 Cut off the cup-shaped compartments of an egg carton. Use a clay pick to poke a hole through the bottom of each cup, in the center.

2 Paint each egg cup orange.

3 Cut a piece of thin wire and thread it through the holes in the painted cups, alternating one cup upward, the next cup downward.

4 Cut the top of the egg carton into seven long strips. Poke a hole with the clay pick at the end of each strip.

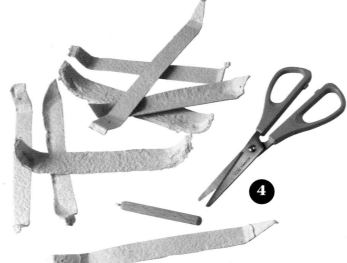

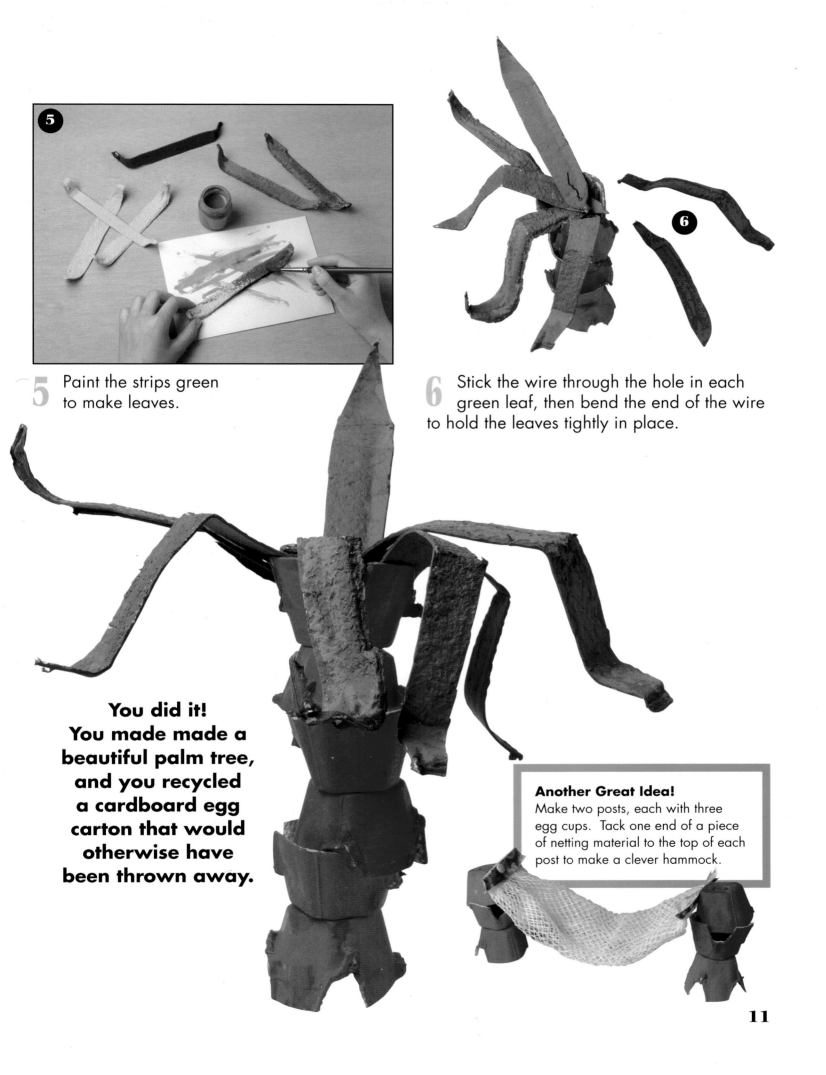

5 Paint the strips green to make leaves.

6 Stick the wire through the hole in each green leaf, then bend the end of the wire to hold the leaves tightly in place.

You did it! You made made a beautiful palm tree, and you recycled a cardboard egg carton that would otherwise have been thrown away.

Another Great Idea!
Make two posts, each with three egg cups. Tack one end of a piece of netting material to the top of each post to make a clever hammock.

11

Bottle Bowling

A splash of paint recycles six plastic bottles into a colorful bowling game. Be sure to put numbered labels on the bottles so you can keep score.

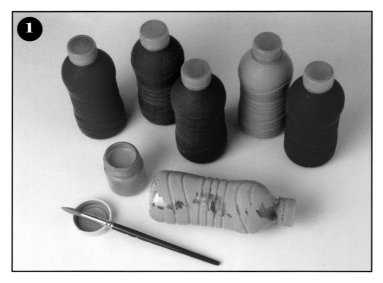

1 Paint each plastic bottle a different color. Use bright colors, such as red, yellow, blue, orange, purple, and green. Do not paint the bottle caps.

2 Cut six strips of white paper to make labels. Each strip should be long enough to fit around a bottle. Using colored pencils, make a very thick number, 1 to 6, on each label.

You will need:
- different colors of acrylic paint
- paintbrush
- 6 plastic bottles
- scissors
- white paper
- colored pencils
- clear tape
- cardboard egg carton
- large bowl

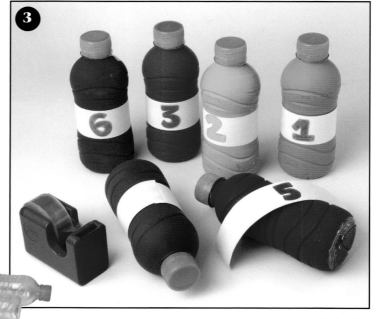

3 Use clear tape to attach a paper label to each bottle.

4 Soak the bottom half of a cardboard egg carton in water until it softens.

5 Roll the wet carton into a ball, squeezing it hard to remove as much water as possible so the ball holds together.

6 Once the ball is dry, paint it green and decorate it with red and white polka dots.

Another Great Idea!
Use modeling clay to make the ball, or use any small ball, instead of making one.

**Put the pins in position . . .
Roll the ball . . . STRIKE!**

Movie Machine

Show your homemade movies on a homemade movie machine. Playing with a cardboard box has never been more fun!

1 Paint the outside of a long, thin, rectangular box light green.

2 Using a black marker and a ruler, draw a rectangle on one of the two large sides of the box, leaving a wide border around the edge of the box. Poke through the marker lines with a clay pick to cut out the center piece.

3 At each end of the two long sides of the box, trace a small circle around the end of a thin cardboard tube.

4 Use a clay pick to punch out the circles, making holes for the cardboard tubes.

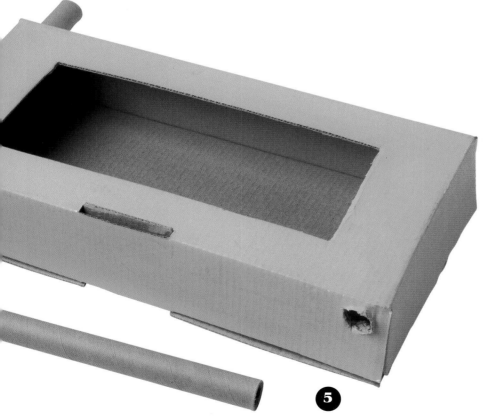

5 Stick a cardboard tube through the holes at each end of the box. The tubes should stick out on each side of the box (as shown).

6 Cut a piece of white paper in half, lengthwise. Tape the two pieces together at their short ends.

7 Draw a series of pictures that tell a story across the length of the paper strip.

8 Color the drawings with colored pencils.

9 Open the box and, on the inside of it, tape one end of the paper strip to one of the cardboard tubes. Be sure the pictures on the paper strip are facing downward.

10 Turn the cardboard tube, rolling the paper strip onto it, until you can tape the end of the strip to the other cardboard tube.

**Lights. Camera. Action!
Turn the cardboard tubes
to show your movie.**

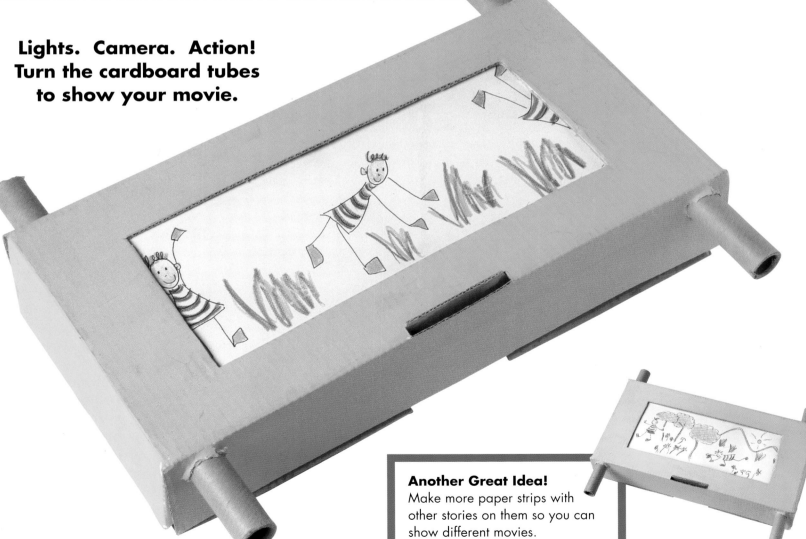

Another Great Idea!
Make more paper strips with other stories on them so you can show different movies.

Simple Stampers

Making your own number stamps is as easy as 1, 2, 3, 4, 5 — five simple steps to make five simple stampers.

You will need:
- clay pick
- scissors
- Styrofoam tray
- red marker
- pencil
- glue stick
- 5 corks
- paintbrush
- different colors of paint
- white paper

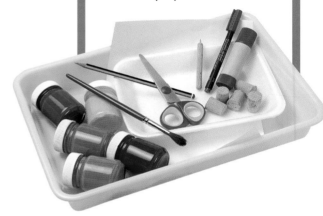

1. Cut out five square pieces from a Styrofoam tray. (Cutting the Styrofoam is easier if you outline the pieces with a clay pick first, then finish cutting with scissors.) With a red marker, draw a number, 1 to 5, on each Styrofoam square. Draw the numbers backward so they will be in the correct position when you stamp them.

2. Press down hard with a pencil as you trace over each number to carve it out more. Decorate the edges of the squares by making small holes with a clay pick.

3. Use a glue stick to attach a cork to the back of each piece of Styrofoam.

18

④

4 Using a different color for each stamp, brush a coat of paint around the number, covering the entire bottom surface of the square.

⑤

5 Stamp the numbers onto a piece of white paper.

Stamp numbers on wood or cardboard — fabric, too. What to stamp is up to you!

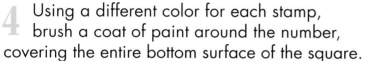

Another Great Idea!
Draw alphabet letters, instead of numbers, or draw flowers, boats, or any other figures you like. Stamp your numbers, letters, or figures on an old white T-shirt to make your own clothing designs.

Cardboard Concertina

**If you have a round cardboard container, don't throw it out!
It's just the right recyclable for making this colorful little accordion.**

1 Paint both parts of a round cardboard container red, inside and out. When the red paint is dry, paint a decorative border of white triangles and green dots on the outside of each part of the container.

2 Cut two strips of red paper, making them as wide as the inside diameter of the container. With a glue stick, glue the short ends of the strips together. Repeat this step with strips of green paper.

You will need:

- red, white, and green paints
- paintbrush
- round cardboard container
- scissors
- red and green construction paper
- ruler
- glue stick
- 2 corks
- liquid school glue

3 To fold the red and green strips together, place the end of one strip at a right angle to the other, then fold one strip on top of the other, over and over, to make an accordion.

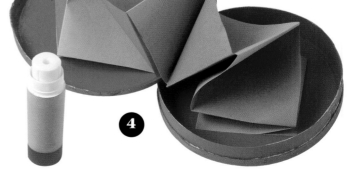

4 Glue the ends of the accordion to the inside of each part of the container.

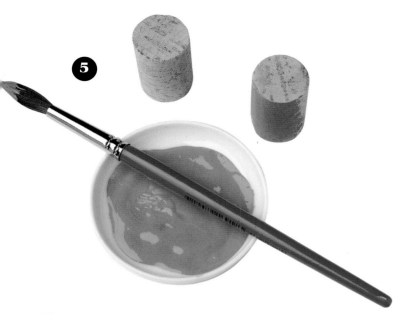

5 Paint two corks green.

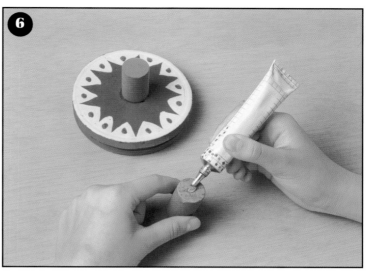

6 With liquid school glue, attach one cork to the center of the decorated side on each part of the container. The corks are the concertina's handles.

To play your concertina, hold each end by its cork handle, then open and close the two parts of the container.

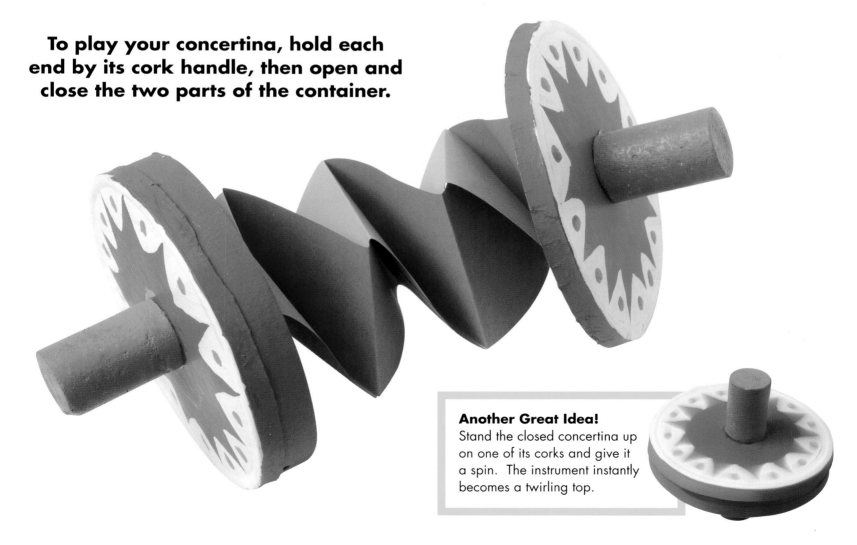

Another Great Idea!
Stand the closed concertina up on one of its corks and give it a spin. The instrument instantly becomes a twirling top.

Jumbo Jet

You can't make a very good paper airplane out of paper towels, but you can use the cardboard tube inside the roll to make this airworthy jet.

You will need:
- black marker
- cardboard
- scissors
- cardboard paper towel tube
- clay pick
- cardboard egg carton
- yellow, green, white, and black paints
- paintbrushes

1 Draw the wings and tail of an airplane on a piece of cardboard, then cut them out.

2 Draw lines on a cardboard paper towel tube, marking where to cut slits in the tube for the wings and tail of the jet. Cut along the lines, first with a clay pick, then with scissors.

3 Slide the wings and the tail pieces into the correct slits on the tube.

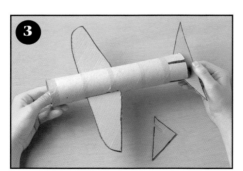

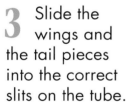

4 Cut one cup off of a cardboard egg carton.

5 Push the egg-carton cup, open end first, into the front end of the paper towel tube so that most of the cup remains outside the tube.

22

6 Paint the entire plane yellow, then add green accents.

7 Paint the windows white with a black outline.

Your plane is ready to fly!

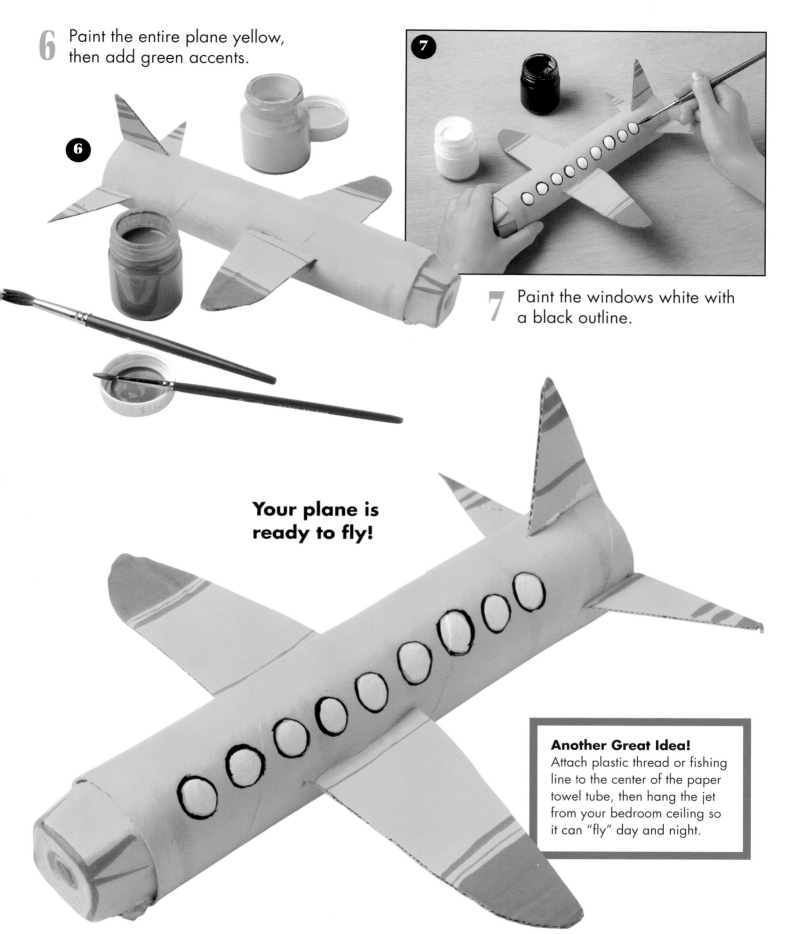

Another Great Idea!
Attach plastic thread or fishing line to the center of the paper towel tube, then hang the jet from your bedroom ceiling so it can "fly" day and night.

Magic Hat

How can two people wear one hat at the same time? Make this magic hat to learn the secret.

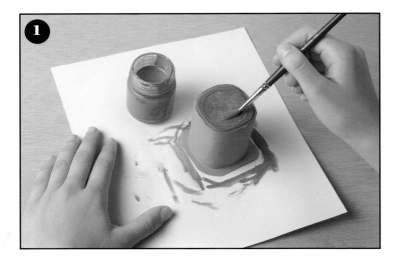

1 Paint a plastic yogurt cup green.

2 When the green paint is dry, decorate the cup with dots of white and red paints.

You will need:

- green, white, and red paints
- paintbrush
- plastic yogurt cup
- white paper
- cardboard toilet paper tube
- black marker
- colored pencils
- glue stick

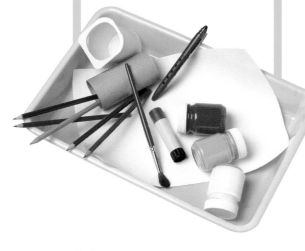

3 Cut a piece of white paper to a size just big enough to wrap around a toilet paper tube. Before gluing the paper onto the tube, draw two faces on it with black marker and colored pencils. Draw one face directly above the other, with one face right side up and the other upside down.

4 Wrap your drawing around the cardboard tube, using a glue stick to attach it.

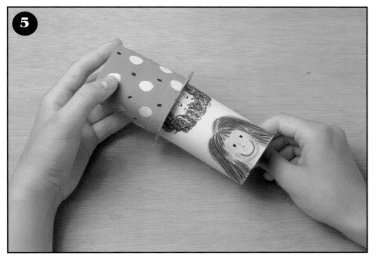

5 Slide the yogurt container over one end of the tube, covering one of the faces. The other face will look as if it is wearing a hat.

You can change the face wearing the hat — like magic! Just slide the hat over the opposite end of the tube.

Another Great Idea!
Cover the yogurt container with decorated colored paper, instead of painting it. If you put a sock over your hand, you can use the magic hat as a puppet. The sock becomes the puppet's dress.

Pretty Purple Purse

Reuse a foil-lined milk or juice carton to make this practical purse. It's a good place to save your pennies and a great way to help the environment.

You will need:

- scissors
- foil-lined milk carton
- purple paper
- glue stick
- yellow poster board
- black marker
- green paint
- paintbrush
- clear tape
- green plastic notebook divider
- self-adhesive Velcro

1 Cut off one of the long, thin sides of a foil-lined milk carton.

2 Wrap a strip of purple paper around the carton. Use a glue stick to attach the paper to the carton.

3 On yellow poster board, draw a semicircle, for the flap of the purse, and cut it out. The diameter of the semicircle should match the length of the milk carton.

4 Paint green dots along the rounded edge of the yellow semicircle to decorate the flap.

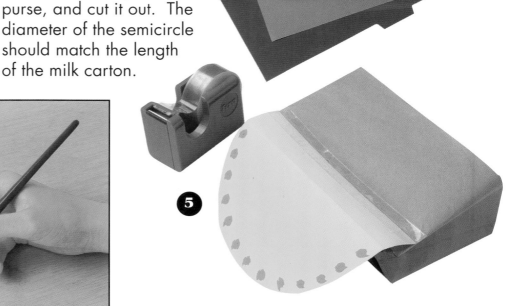

5 Tape the flap to the back of the milk carton so that you can fold it over the open side of the carton like a cover.

26

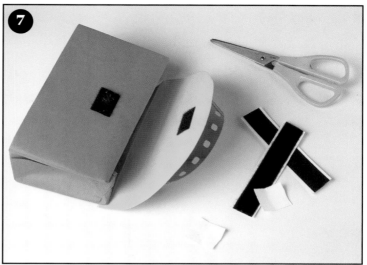

6 To make a handle for the purse, cut the strip of holes off of a green plastic notebook divider and attach the strip to the back of the purse with tape.

7 For a clasp, stick small pieces of self-adhesive Velcro to the front of the purse and to the inside of the flap.

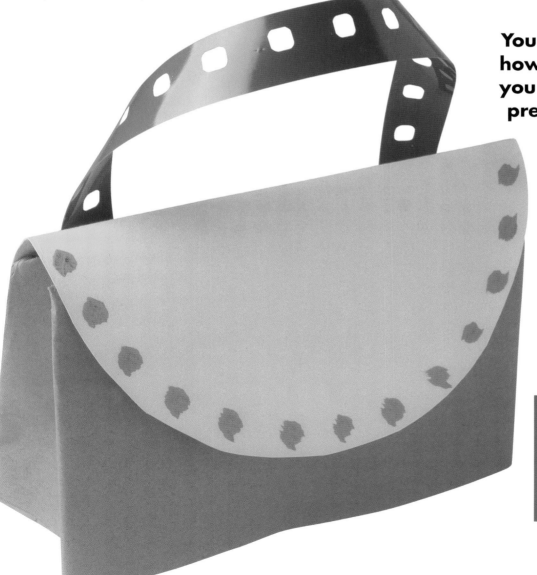

You'll be surprised at how many "pennies" you can carry in your pretty purple purse.

Another Great Idea!
Leave the handle off to make a clutch bag, and decorate the flap with a flower for a different look.

Baby Bear

An empty chocolate pudding cup is just the throwaway you need to make a cute little nose for this baby bear's face.

1 Draw the shape of a bear's face and ears on orange poster board and cut it out.

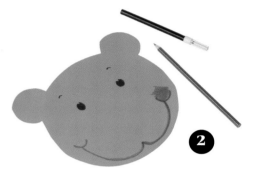

2 With a black marker and a red colored pencil, draw on eyes, a mouth, and cheeks.

You will need:
- black marker
- orange poster board
- scissors
- red colored pencil
- Styrofoam tray
- glue stick
- brown plastic pudding cup
- liquid school glue

3 Draw two ears on a Styrofoam tray and cut them out. Make these ears smaller than the ears on the bear's face.

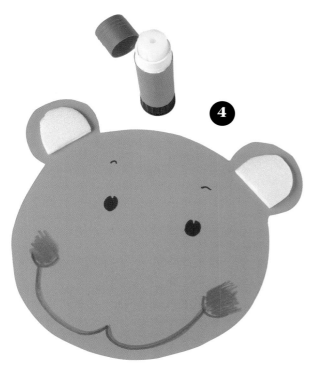

4 Place the Styrofoam ears over the ears on the bear's face, using a glue stick to attach them.

5 Round the top edge of a pudding cup by trimming off the corners with scissors. With liquid school glue, glue the pudding cup upside down in the center of the bear's face to make its nose.

With its nose in a pudding cup, what little bear wouldn't have a big smile on its face.

Another Great Idea!
Use a plastic container of a different shape and color to make the nose of another animal, such as a pink pig.

Potted Posy

You can do so much more than drink with a plastic cup and a straw. Watch how easily you can transform them into a decorative flower.

You will need:
- Popsicle sticks
- plastic food storage container
- yellow, red, and green paints
- paintbrush
- liquid school glue
- red marker
- yellow plastic notebook divider
- scissors
- red plastic cup
- green paper
- clear tape
- straw

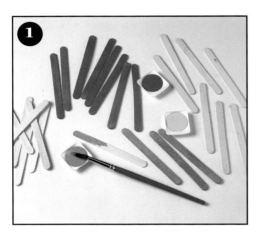

1 Gather enough Popsicle sticks to cover a plastic food storage container. Paint some of the sticks yellow, some of them red, and some green.

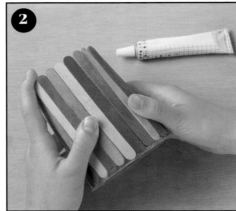

2 Use liquid school glue to attach the painted sticks to the outside of the container. Alternate the three colors of the sticks as you glue them on.

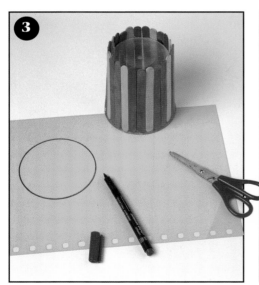

3 Use a red marker to trace around the opening of the container on a yellow plastic notebook divider, then cut out the circle.

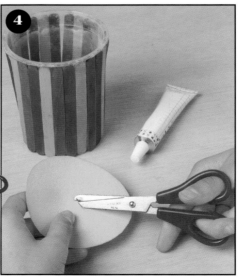

4 With the tip of a scissors, make a small slit in the center of the circle. Glue the circle to the top of the container as if it were a cover.

5 To make a flower, cut the sides of a red plastic cup into strips, rounding the ends. Fold the strips outward, one at a time.

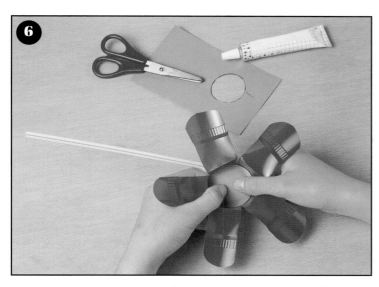

6 Cut a circle out of green paper and glue it to the bottom of the red cup, which has become the center of the flower.

7 Tape a straw to the back of the flower to make a stem.

This posy is always in bloom — and you never have to water it!

8 Stick the end of the straw through the slit in the cover of the flowerpot.

Another Great Idea!
Cut several slits into the cover of the container to make a toothbrush holder. Putting heavy objects, such as marbles, into the container, before you cover it, will keep it from tipping over.

Glossary

accents: added details or decorations that improve the appearance of a main object

alternating: arranging something in a repeating pattern

clasp: **(n)** a fastener that, like a snap or a button, holds something closed

clutch bag: a purse, or handbag, that does not have a strap or a handle on it

concertina: a musical instrument that looks like a small accordion

diameter: the distance across the center of a circle

dilute: make thinner or more fluid, usually by mixing with water or another liquid

flexible: able to be bent

posy: flower

self-adhesive: able to stick to another surface without using glue or tape

twine: a type of strong string made out of strands of material that are twisted together

Velcro: the trademark name for a type of fastener that holds items together when tiny nylon hooks on one side are pressed against soft nylon loops on the other side

More Books to Read

Cardboard Tube Mania. Christine M. Irvin (Children's Book Press)

Crafts from Junk. Step by Step (series). Violaine Lamerand (Bridgestone Books)

Creative Crafts from Cardboard Boxes. Nikki Conner (Copper Beech Books)

Fun with Recycling: 50 Great Things for Kids to Make from Junk. Marion Elliot (Southwater)

Look What You Can Make with Plastic Foam Trays. Kelly Milner Halls (Boyds Mills Press)

Milk Carton Mania. Christine M. Irvin (Children's Book Press)

Web Sites

Kids Domain: Reusing Materials to Make New Crafts. www.kidsdomain.com/craft/_recycle.html

Trash to Treasure: A fun way to recycle! craftsforkids.miningco.com/library/bltrashtr.htm